FIRE TV ST

2019 COMPLETE USER GUIDE AND HOW TO JAILBREAK YOUR DEVICE + OVER 100 TIPS & TRICKS

Tech Reviewer

TABLE OF CONTENT

Introduction to the Amazon Fire TV Stick

The Fire TV Stick is one of Amazon's most demanded and popular products. This incredible device is one of the most used streaming technologies in the market. It runs on the same operating system as the Fire TV, the Fire tablet, Amazon Echo devices and the Fire Stick 4k.

This book would guide you on how to use your device from unboxing, setting-up, modifying settings, troubleshooting common issues and jailbreaking your Fire Tv Stick. It also includes tips on how to stream content smoothly and the best apps to install for a fantastic streaming experience as well as several tricks designed to give more freedom in the fire stick device. It is a must read for every fire stick user.

What is a Fire TV Stick?

The Amazon Fire TV Stick is a miniature media device that bears a striking resemblance to a USB flash drive. It is activated after it is plugged into the HDMI port usually located at the back of the television set.

After the purchase of your fire stick, you get to see the accessories that comes with it in the pack. These include the fire stick device itself, a power cable, adapter, HDMI extension cable, a pair of Amazon batteries, a user's guide and a remote.

The fire Stick is a media device that enables any television set with a HDMI port to connect to the internet and stream contents directly from Netflix, YouTube, HBO, Pandora, Hulu etc.

The Amazon fire TV stick gives you access to online media content such as television shows, series, photos, games, news and music. It opens your television set to a vast world of information and entertainment far beyond what your conventional television can provide.

Technical Details of the Amazon Fire TV Stick

Size: (85.9mm x 30.0mm x 12.6mm)

Weight: 32 grams

Processor: MediaTek Quad Core ARM 1.3 GHz

GPU: Mali450

Bluetooth: Yes, 4.1 version

Wi-Fi: 802.11 ac

Video Output Resolution: 720/1080p

RAM: 1 gigabyte

ROM: 8 gigabytes

Voice Support: Yes (optional)

How Does the Fire TV Stick Work?

The fire stick has to be set up first before it can function. A comprehensive guide on the procedure to set up the fire TV stick has been written below under the subhead; "Setting Up the Fire Stick". The Amazon fire stick operates in a similar way as Roku and Chromecast, its rivals in streaming technology. Once you have set up the fire stick and logged into your Amazon account, you can easily access the content purchased from your Amazon account. You can also view photos uploaded to the Amazon cloud service.

The fire stick is a central storage for all the media content you wish to access online. To have a pleasurable gaming experience on the fire stick for game lovers, you need to get the controller which is available for purchase on the Amazon store. Exciting apps like HBO, Hulu and ESPN allows you to access your preferred channels and apps with Pluto TV, IMDb Freedive, and others.

Unboxing the Fire Stick

The fire stick comes in a micro box like other devices. Follow the steps below to unveil your new device;

- Take off the plastic cover on the pack.
- Gently cut through the sealed spot at the top of the pack using a sharp object like a letter opener, knife or blade.

Setting Up the Fire Stick

The next step is to set up the fire stick. To successfully set up your fire Tv stick, you need the following which would not be included in the box:

- An Amazon account. If the Fire Stick was bought from your Amazon account, it is automatically linked to your account and so you can access everything you have on your Amazon account. If you received it as a gift, you would need to sign up on www.amazon.com to create an account and enjoy your device.
- Strong Wi-fi network connection.

- A television set that is compatible with the Amazon fire TV stick either the HD or UHD and must have a HDMI port. You would attach the HDMI extension in the HDMI port.

Now that these components have been outlined in details, let's get you to the step by step procedure in setting up the Amazon TV Fire Stick;

Set Up Procedure; Step by Step

- With your Fire Stick device, you will see a HDMI and a micro-USB port. Attach your USB power cord to the micro-USB in the Fire Stick while the other end of the power cord goes to the Power Adapter.
- Plug the adapter to a power outlet
- Plug in your fire stick to the HDMI port which is located at the back of the television set. This is not the only way to

8

connect the fire stick to the television set. That is a direct connection. If you don't want to plug the fire stick directly, you can use the HDMI extension and then you plug the fire stick to one end of the extension cable and the other end of the cable gets connected to the HDMI port. Note down the number for the HDMI port you used as you would need to turn on the matching HDMI number Channel on your TV.

- Switch on the Fire Stick.
- Locate the correct port and input the fire stick. If it's in the wrong port, the screen won't respond to the device.
- Use the remote. You first of all, insert the batteries to power the remote which instantly pairs with the fire stick when it comes on. If it fails to pair with the fire stick when it is powered on, press the home button and hold for a few seconds.

The remote launches into discovery mode to complete the pairing with the fire stick.

- Click "Home" on your remote
- Click "Play/Pause" on your remote
- Proceed to choose the language you desire
- Select the Wi-Fi network you want to connect to, enter password and connect to the wireless network.
- After you are connected, go back to the main settings and scroll right to the Account settings, select "Register" account if you have an existing Amazon account or "Create an account" if you do not have an account with Amazon.
- Enter your login details then click next. If you want to create account, you will be creating your login identification at this point.
- Type in your password then sign in. If you have the two-factor authentication

enabled, confirmation code will be sent to your registered phone number which you would input to continue with registration.

- After that is done, you will be asked to confirm it's your account, go ahead to confirm.

- Another question will pop up to confirm if you want to store the Wi-fi connection password on your Amazon account, choose yes or no to opt in or out.

- Proceed to either enable or disable parental controls.

- On the next screen, accept to sign up for Prime account or decline.

- Next screen would ask you to choose the apps you wish to download. You will see "Choose Apps" and "No, thanks". You can click choose apps if you want to visit the Amazon store and see apps you can download to your device or you click "No, thanks" to skip.

- Various streaming services such as Hulu, HBO, Direct TV now will pop up, you choose the ones you are interested in then click right to proceed to TV channels.
- Select your desired television channels app then proceed to Sports apps.
- After selecting the Sports apps, click right to proceed to featured apps.
- Pick the featured apps you need at the time and then you select "play" to proceed
- Then you proceed to download all the selected apps. Fire stick has been set and is ready to entertain and inform you.

Fire Stick Settings

After the unboxing and setting up process of the fire stick, the next thing to do is the device settings. Every gadget comes with settings. In order to know how to fully enjoy, operate and customize your experience with this digital wonder, you need to familiarize yourself with the settings. Although, the fire stick device has been programmed to configure settings automatically, users can still modify these settings. I will show you how.

Every setting has a menu. To access the settings for this device, you press and hold the home button for the menu to come up and you select "settings".

The settings menu will pop up and you will see various categories of settings.

Different Settings on the Fire TV Stick

1. **Notifications Settings**

There you get messages about system applications and updates. You can modify your notifications to your taste and preference.

Notifications can get irritating, so it's necessary one learns how to customize, monitor and stop such notifications when necessary.

Some users may not like the idea of getting notifications while they are viewing their streamed content as it could interrupt or distract them. So am going to give you tips or steps on how to switch off notifications;

Starting from the home screen, go to Settings, click the Notifications icon.

Under the notifications, choose the "Settings" option, then you select "Preferences". You can change the notification settings of all applications on your fire stick device. Simply put, you can modify the settings to continue receiving notification updates on certain apps and discontinue reception of updates on others.

Under the notification settings of these applications, you will see the option "Do not interrupt", you toggle it to off to turn off pop-up notifications settings for all applications.

To turn off notification on select applications, click on "App Notifications" so you can have a view of all the apps installed on your fire stick device.

Select the apps you want to switch off notifications for then switch off notification for each of the individual apps.

2. Network Settings

Network settings is the second icon on the settings menu. There you will see options like "All networks", "Other networks" and "Join network using WPS". Here, you can modify your connection to the internet. Here are tips on how to operate network settings.

Use the navigational buttons on the remote, click down then right to highlight the "Network" option in yellow, then you click the middle button to select, this activates the device Wi-Fi to start searching for nearby networks.

You will see your home network come up among the list of nearby networks. Use your remote navigational buttons to highlight your home network in yellow and then click the middle button to select it. If you don't see your home network, click "rescan" at the bottom of the network list. In a case your home networks doesn't pop up because it is hidden, select "join other networks" also at the bottom of the network list and type in the name of the network you want to connect to.

If your home network is not locked, your fire stick device will proceed to connect. If it's locked, you will need to input your Wi-Fi password to access your home network. To do that, use your remote navigations to access your on-screen keyboard and then type in your password.

After you input your password, you will see the option to "connect" at the lower right of the on-screen keyboard. Select it. You are connected to the network.

3. Display & Sounds Settings

This is the third settings on the settings menu. There you will see sub-options such as "Enable Display Mirroring", "HDMI CEC control" and "Second Screen Notifications". Here, you can modify your visual and audio settings. Such settings come in handy when your picture doesn't display perfectly and you need to adjust it to screen size.

How to Modify Display?

- From the home screen, you go to **Settings** then go to **"Display & Sounds"** which is the third settings on the settings menu. Click **"Display"** under the settings.

- You will see **"Calibrate display"** under it, use the up and down keys to arrange the arrows and ensure that they are in sync with the borders of your screen.

- Click **"Accept"** then go back to see if the adjustment has been effected.

- Display and sounds settings help users to regulate audio settings, view television specifications, put up a screen saver and configure television display style.

How to Disable Navigational Sounds on Your Remote

Just like a cellular device, every fire stick remote gives off clicking sound by default. This could irritate users. Below are tips on how to switch it off;

- Under the Settings menu, click on "Display and Sounds"
- Next screen would request for your 4-digit Amazon Video Pin, input it.
- Then select "Audio" option.
- Select "Navigation sounds", switch it off.

4. **Applications Settings**

The fourth icon is the Applications icon. Here, you get to see sub-options such as "Collect App usage data", "Prime Photos", "Game Circle" and "Appstore", and "Manage Installed Applications". Here, you can view and manage your applications, install, update, disable updates for apps and remove apps as well.

How to Install Apps on Fire Stick?

- Under applications settings, proceed to the "**Appstore**" section.

- There, you can search for the kind of apps you desire to purchase
- Select to "Get Now", "Buy Now" or "Download" the app

How to Remove Apps on Fire Stick?

- Go to Settings, then Applications.
- You will see "Manage Installed Applications"
- Click that option and you will view all your apps; you select the app you want to remove.
- Once the options pop up, select Uninstall.
- A confirmation screen would pop up, select Uninstall again

How to Update the Fire Stick?

- Go to Settings.
- Navigate to "My Fire TV"
- Click "About"

- Select "**Check for System update** "

How to Automatically Update Apps on Fire Stick?

- To automatically update apps on your fire stick device, do the following;
- Under Application Settings, go to Appstore.
- Go to "Automatic updates" and toggle it to on.
- How to Manually Update Individual Apps
- From the home screen, go to the App menu at the right-hand side of the screen.
- The apps on the device would come up, use your remote to navigate to the app you wish to update.
- You would see an Update button if there is any available update for that app.
- Click on the Update button.
- A popup will appear with two option; Update App Now or Update Later.

- Select Update App Now. This would automatically update the app to the most current version.
- Once the update is complete, the app will launch by itself.

How to Disable App Updates on Fire Stick?

- Go to applications settings, select "Appstore"
- Select "Automatic updates" and switch it off.

5. Controllers & Bluetooth Devices Settings

Here you see sub options such as "Game Controls", "Amazon fire remotes" and "Other Bluetooth devices". Here, you manage remotes, Bluetooth devices and controllers.

How to Connect the Fire Stick to your Bluetooth Device?

- Go to Settings, then Controller and Bluetooth Devices, chose other "Bluetooth devices" option.
- Chose "Add Bluetooth devices"
- Once that is done, your fire stick will start searching for nearby Bluetooth devices, wait for it to locate your Bluetooth device, then you select it once it shows and wait for the pairing process to be complete.
- Once this is done, the audio output will automatically transfer from the fire stick to the paired device.

This very same process also works for gamers who want to experience gaming on their television sets via the fire stick. The same pairing process for Bluetooth devices also applies to game controllers.

6. Alexa App Settings

The sixth icon is the Alexa (voice control) logo. In this menu, the user can manage the Alexa app and use it to customize his or her Alexa experience. It contains sub-options such as "Alexa App" and "Things to try".

Connecting to Alexa

Alexa is Amazon's voice control feature and it is the brain behind a host of devices such as the Fire TV, the Fire Stick, Amazon Echo devices, the Fire tablet and other third-party devices with the Alexa smart voice user interface.

Alexa's functionality is phenomenal. It can be used to control cameras, door locks, home theatre, navigate across devices. Devices that are connected to Alexa increases customer's awareness of the engagements of a smart device.

Top Features

1. Complete Voice User Interface

Heard of Alexa's native smart home voice user interface? It makes customer adoption easier. This voice interface contains a lot of voice commands that covers a good number of the device's functionalities.

However, if there are certain commands you want to be there that are not there by default, you can customize the commands and add the ones you want. This modification doesn't in any way disturb the fantastic experience that's a consequence of the Alexa voice feature.

2. Few Barriers to Customer Adoption

Users with Alexa can control any endpoint on their device. By endpoints, am referring to devices such as the Fire TV, Echo, Echo Show and a vast array of third-party devices with the Alexa software.

3. Complete and Fun Experience with Multiple Devices

Alexa "Routines" and "Groups" make this possible. They help by simplifying the user's usage of the devices. With "Routines" helps users trigger a series of actions in one or more devices by a single command. It can also be triggered by another device trigger, the time of the day or change in sensor. With "Groups", as long as there is an echo device in the same room as the other device, that device stays connected.

4. Connectivity Options

There are multiple options for Alexa to connect with your device.

A. Locally

You can use smart home hubs such as ZigBee to connect Alexa to devices like Fire stick.

B. Via the Cloud

Your fire stick device has a cloud. You can use Smart Home and Custom Skill APIs to connect your device cloud to Alexa. When the user wants to use Alexa to control the device, the cloud sends instructions to the device through the internet.

C. On the Device

This connection can be done by using the Alexa Connect Kit (ACK). As Alexa communicates with the ACK module over the internet, it uses a serial interface to sends those voice instructions to your device.

How to Connect Alexa to Your Fire Tv

If there is only one Fire Tv linked to your Amazon account, Alexa would automatically complete the linking process. Follow the steps below to link Alexa to your device if you have multiple Fire TV:

- Open the Alexa App on your device. To do this, click on the Alexa Icon.
- Click the Menu button (this is the 3 horizontal lines in the left upper side of the screen. This would show you the different options in the Alexa app.
- Click on Music, Videos and Books.
- On the next screen, select the Fire TV options from the list on the screen.
- Next, select Link Your Alexa Device. This would connect Alexa to your Fire TV.
- Next screen would bring up all your available Fire TV devices, chose the device you want to connect to Alexa, then click on Continue.

- The next screen would bring up list of all your devices connected to Alexa, each with a checkbox. Here, chose all the devices you would want to use to control your Fire TV. Once done, click the Link Devices option.

- You would see an up to date list of all the devices linked in the app, from here, you can either unlink a device or link a new Fire TV to Alexa.

- Hold the Home button for some seconds under the Settings option comes up.

- From the options, click on 'Alexa'

- Select Alexa App to design your Alexa moments.

How to Use Your Alexa Voice Remote

- To use Alexa command, press and hold the **Voice** 🎤 button on your Fire TV stick and ask Alexa for anything you want Alexa to do for you.

- Once you make the command, Alexa responds via your Fire TV. Several features pop up in different displays on your screen.
- To return to the previous screen when you an Alexa display on your screen, simply press the **Back** ⊖ or **Home** ⊙ buttons

The following are some of the features you can control on your TV using Alexa:

To do this on your Fire TV	Say this to Alexa
Play a TV show or a movie	Watch (title) Play (title or genre)
Search for TV shows and movies	Search for (name of TV show or movie) Show me titles with

	(name of author)
Search within apps	Show me (movie name or TV show Search for (name of program)
Control Playback	Play/ Pause Resume/ Stop Rewind/ Fast forward etc
Live TV controls	Go to (name of Network/ Channels) Watch (name of Network or channels)

Launch Apps from your Games and Apps	Open/ Launch
Return to Fire TV home screen	Go Home

7. Preferences Settings

The seventh icon on the settings menu is the Preferences. This has many sub-options. **"Parental controls","** **Notification settings",** **"Featured Contents", "Time zone", "Language",** **"Advertising ID" and "Metric Units".** All these can be managed and modified according to the preferences of the user.

How to Set up Parental Controls on Fire Stick?

- Under Settings>Preferences, "Parental Control" is the first option

- Select it and then enable it.
- Parental controls help restrict access to data, in-app purchasing etc.

How to Set Up Featured Content Settings on Fire Stick?

Although you cannot remove or put off the featured content section, however, every option under the preferences settings can easily be modified. All the sub   options are highlighted there. All you have to is just click it and select whatever modifications suit your taste.

- Go to Settings from the menu
- Select Preferences then chose Featured Content.
- Set **"Allow Video AutoPlay"** to OFF, for the featured content section to show still images alone.

- Switch off the **"Allow Audio AutoPlay"** option for the video clips in this section to play without sound.

8. Device Settings

The eighth icon is the Device icon. Under this, we have "About", "Developer options", "Legal and Compliance", "Sleep", "Restart" and 'Reset to Factory defaults". This menu option contains information on your fire stick device. Here, you can control the device settings and fire it up by restarting it whenever necessary.

How to Enable Apps from Unknown Sources on Your Fire Stick

- From the settings menu, proceed to the "Device" settings
- Under device settings, select "Developer Options"

- Under that, select "Apps from Unknown Sources", you switch to on.

How to Sleep your Fire Stick Device?

The fire stick device has been programmed to go to sleep if left idle for a certain period of time but there are settings to ensure you can sleep your device whenever you want.

- Press the home button for about 3-4 seconds, you will see the quick access menu pop up on your TV screen.
- Select "Sleep" on the quick access menu and your screen will turn black.

How to Restart Your Fire Stick?

There are two options available to restart your Fire Stick, they are;

Using the Fire Stick Remote

- Hold the select button and the play/pause button at the same time for about five seconds until your device restarts.

Using the Power Source

- Unplug the power adaptor from the power source for about three seconds.
- Plug it back, the device will restart.

How to Reset Factory Defaults on Your Fire Stick?

There are various ways to reset your Fire TV Stick. They are

Factory Reset Fire Tv Stick Using Remote

- From the settings menu, you go right and click on My Fire TV.
- Select "Reset to Factory Defaults" from the pop-up options on the screen.

- You will see a dialog box, to confirm your request to reset the device. Click on Reset.
- The system would begin the process to reset your device which should take about 5 to 8 minutes. Ensure you do not remove the Fire Stick nor turn off the TV during this process.
- Your Fire Stick will restart and you would see a screen reading "Resetting your Fire Stick"
- Next is a prompt to connect to your Wi-fi network, once the network is connected, you would see the Amazon sign-in screen.

Using Remote Buttons

Sometimes you may be unable to see the screen because of black screen or frozen system. In times like this, your Fire Stick remote would work for factory reset.

Note: The Fire TV Stick has to be paired to the remote for this to work. If using a new remote, restart the Fire Stick and hold the home button for approximately 20 seconds for the stick to pair with the remote.

To carry out the factory reset, press and hold both the right and back buttons of your remote for a minimum of 10 seconds to begin the reset process. Follow the instructions on the screen to finish the process.

Use Another Remote

If you do not have your remote available but have a friend or family member using same Fire Stick, you can pair their remote with your Fire TV Stick then follow the steps above.

Use Your TV Remote

To use your TV remote to control your Fire TV stick, you need to enable the CEC settings in your

TV. Different TVs have their different name and locations.

Factory Reset without Remote and Wi-fi

What happens in cases where you do not have a remote available or your TV doesn't support CEC and the Wi-Fi connection for your app is different. You have no worries. Just make the Fire TV Stick to believe you are using the old Wi-Fi network. To do this, you can either edit the router name and password to the details of the last network the Fire TV Stick used or let your mobile phone serve as a hotspot connection using same name and password as the previous Wi-Fi network.

This way, your phone and your Fire TV Stick would connect to the same Wi-Fi. Then access the Fire TV app on your phone to get to the controls and reset your device.

9. Accessibility Settings

The ninth icon is **Accessibility**. This has the options of "Closed Caption", "VoiceView" and "High Contrast Text". Here, you can alter texts in black or white, manage VoiceView which is a screen layer for fire stick devices. You can also turn on captioning.

VoiceView

This is a fire stick feature that enables textual content on screen to have audio output. For instance, if you are using your remote to navigate across the fire stick interface, VoiceView simply say out loud what activities you are doing, which app you are running, which modifications you are making and so on. To switch on or switch off this feature, the user is required to press the back button and the menu button simultaneously for three seconds. A tutorial on how to use the

VoiceView would come up when you first access this feature.

Closed Captions

This feature is concerned with subtitles for both video content and audio output in English and any other languages supported by the fire stick device. For movies and shows that have subtitle available, you would see the CC symbol in the details of the video.

To Watch Videos or TV Shows with Subtitles

- Start Video Playback
- Click the menu button on your remote to display extra options for the video playback
- You will see "Subtitles and Audio", proceed to select.
- Click the "On" button under "Subtitles and Captions", then click any of the

available language from the options on the screen to put on the Captions.

- Tip: You can choose how you want the subtitles to show, from text size and style. A sample of your choice would show on the screen.
- After that is done, click the Menu ⊜ button again to exit those settings and resume playback with subtitles.
- To switch off subtitles, tap the Menu button, open the Subtitles and Audio again, select the captions options you currently have enabled, then an option to set the subtitles to Off will show.

High Contrast Text

This is an experimental feature on the fire stick device. It's basic purpose to enhance readability of text on the screen by displaying them in black and white. It is one of the options under the "Accessibility" section of settings. The user can easily switch it off and on from there. However, this feature could be a reason you have some navigational issues or problems with certain selections.

10. Help and Support Settings

The tenth icon is the **Help or Support** icon. Here, you can get relevant information whenever you have an issue with the device. Sub-options include "Help Videos", "Feedback", "Quick Tips" and "Contact Us".

Help Videos

They are relevant videos that users of the fire stick will find useful. They contain information and show users especially the new users how to do certain things on their fire stick device, such as settings and modifications, how to install apps, uninstall apps, access music online and so much more.

Feedback

This is one of the options under the "Help and Support" section of settings. Here, the user can express his feelings of his experience of the fire stick device and if it is satisfactory or not.

Quick Tips

This section is dedicated to helping new users get familiar with their fire stick capabilities and settings. On this section, you will get quick information on functions like using Alexa, changing location, using voice search, set up parental controls, turn off advertising, turn off notifications, how to change featured content and so on.

Contact Us

This is the link between the manufacturer and the user. Just like "Feedback". If you want to make an inquiry or you need help trying to fix up your fire TV stick, this is the section that takes care of that. It is required of users to login to their Amazon account and contact Amazon customer support. Here, you can reach the Amazon customer service directly by dialling 1-888-280-4431.

11. Account Settings

The eleventh and final icon is the Account. Here, you have the sub-options of "Amazon Account" and "Sync Amazon Content". This is where you come to register or deregister your device. You can also sync contents like game and videos across all your supported devices.

How to Register Your Account

- To ensure your Amazon account is registered for the full experience, follow these simple settings;
- Go to the settings menu (click the home button and scroll right to the very last icon).
- Click "Account", you will see "Register", click it and follow the instructions you see.

What Happens if I Deregister My Fire Stick Device?

If a user gets his device deregistered, he will lose access to all the Amazon contents and many features that comes with the fire stick will cease to work.

What the Amazon TV Fire Stick Can Do?

This digital delight boasts a variety of functions, some of which have been mentioned sparingly in certain segments of this book but here, they will be discussed in details.

1. Access to Netflix

Yeah! This smart technology brings Netflix to your television screens courtesy it's access to the internet. To connect your device to your Netflix account from your device home screen, follow the steps below:

- On the main screen of your device click the search button and type "Netflix".
- Click the search button.
- From the search results, click on the Netflix app to open.
- Then click on Free or Download button.

- Once its successfully downloaded, click on Sign-in.

- Input your Netflix email and password to sign in into a world of limitless visual entertainment.

Method 2:

In cases where you are unable to get Netflix from the Amazon store, then follow the steps below to get it through Downloader.

- To start, first visit **Settings** > **Device/My Fire TV** > **Developer** on your Fire Stick.

- Go to **ADB Debugging** and enable.

- Also, activate **Apps from Unknown sources** option.

- Then search for Downloader in the search button on your Fire Stick.

- Once the result is in, select the Downloader application.

- Tap Download to begin to download the app to your device.

- Chose the **Open** button once the download is complete.

- In the address bar, put in the Netflix URL to download Netflix into your device.

- Select **Go.** This would download the Netflix apk file.

- Once the download is complete, click **Next.**

- Tap **Install.** And you have Netflix ready.

2. Access to Music Online

The Amazon Fire TV Stick enables users to stream, import and purchase music online. Music lovers should be pleased with this function in particular. If you are using an Amazon Prime account, you can listen to already included music or sign up for subscription to music. Also, if you have an account with Spotify, YouTube, you can access these apps if they are available from the Amazon App store.

3. Voice Control (Alexa)

This is basically what makes the Amazon TV Fire Stick state-of-the-art technology. You can activate this voice control and perform so many functions. You can do various things such as getting an update on the weather forecast, choose a movie on Netflix or any movie Applications you know of, you can even use voice control to order stuffs from online retail stores. We have talked intensively on the Alexa above.

4. Cellular Screen Mirroring

The Fire Stick can put whatever is displaying on your phone on the TV screen. To activate this function, follow the steps below:

- Hold the home button.
- You will be launched into Settings.

- Select the Display and Sounds, select "Mirroring".
- Go to your phone settings, search for the Mirroring Option. This is limited to certain cellular devices.

5. Digital Sync or Signage

This function is for users that wants to share their content on the TV screen via the fire stick. This function is very useful in the world of business and it is a good alternative for those who can't afford to replace their old screens for new, more advanced screens. Digital signage is used in art galleries, exhibitions, event spaces and trade shows.

As long as your television screens has a HDMI port, it can be transformed into a smart TV via the Amazon fire stick. Bottom line, your television set can perform the above function. To set up digital signage on your TV, do this:

- Use the fire stick to download the Screen Cloud App.
- Then you launch the application after download.
- After that, you sign up on the Screen Cloud web app which you have to do via your laptop or PC. You can sign up with your mail account or your Google account.
- After sign up, you log in and click "Add Screens" which pops up, you enter the pairing code and you are automatically synced and in charge of your screen.
- Thereafter, you add content and organize it to your taste or preference.

How Can I Close an Application on Amazon TV Fire Stick?

This is quite simple! Do this:

- Go to the settings menu.

- Click the Applications icon, select the option "Manage installed applications".
- Select the desired app then click "Force Stop"

How to Install and Operate Android Applications on the Amazon Fire Stick?

The Amazon fire stick is based on the Android operating system so it is compatible with Android applications. You can do this through a process called "sideload" where you can get some of the applications from your PC pushed onto the fire stick.

Fire Stick Cache; What are They and How to Clear Them?

Every device user is familiar with slow speeds, app crashes and hitches in performance as a result of accumulated junk data piled from the device's activity over time. Once these starts occurring on your fire stick device, the solution is to clear the cache so the fire stick device keeps performing at optimal level.

Everything downloaded comes with a cache, it is data the device stores while the app or whatever downloaded is operating. A cache needs to be cleared when it gets too large and takes too much space, performance slows down or the application crashes. A cache also needs to be cleared when the cache gets corrupted.

However, it isn't possible to wipe out the entire cache on your device at once. You are limited to clearing the cache of each app one after the other or you just clear the cache of the specific app giving you trouble.

Here is a step by step procedure on how to clear caches on your fire stick devices;

- Click the home button on your Amazon remote to get to the home menu on your screen.
- Proceed to settings
- Proceed to the applications icon
- Proceed to "Manage Installed Applications" option. All the apps you have on the fire stick device will show.
- Select the specific app whose cache you desire to clear.
- Proceed to the clear cache. In any event, step six doesn't solve your issues, proceed to clear data. Certain apps permit their cookies to be cleared.
- If there are more caches to be cleared as regards other apps giving you the same issue, then you go back and repeat the first six steps with the other apps.

How to Free Up Space on your Fire Stick

Apart from clearing caches on your app, there are a few other ways to get rid of excess files on your device. You need to take into consideration the size of each app and the amount of storage space they occupy on your device.

It is advisable to focus on the apps you rarely use. You can either clear their data or you delete the app from the device.

- Press your home button and proceed to settings.
- Go to the device icon
- Select "About" option
- Go to "Storage". Here, you get to see how much space you have left on your device and the apps taking up the greatest number of bytes.
- Go back to the settings menu
- Visit the Applications icon
- Select the "Manage the installed applications" option

- Uninstall the app or clear a bulk of its size by just clearing data or cache.

Troubleshooting Basic and Advanced Problems on the Amazon TV Fire Stick

Every digital device is bound to undergo issues or glitches that will demand troubleshooting. It is more or less, an unwritten law. You may want to ask what exactly is troubleshooting? Troubleshooting is the process of fixing mechanical or technical issues ranging from simple to complex in a machinery or computer.

Every hardware or software issue any device undergoes could be caused by the mishandling of the device as well as other factors. For most of the issues you may encounter with your device, the best and fastest solutions are to restart the device, confirm that the device is connected to a strong internet as well as confirm that the HDMI cable is plugged to the correct HDMI port. We would however, go into details for specific problems you may encounter with your device.

How to Handle Streaming Glitches on the Amazon TV Fire Stick

There is nothing as annoying as getting your connection interrupted especially if you are fully absorbed and concentrated on what you are viewing. It is more of nuisance than an issue to experienced users. It can easily be handled.

There are things to consider when you encounter buffering on your devices. Buffering is another word for streaming glitches. I will be using them interchangeably. We will look at what could be the possible causes of this issue.

Possible Causes and Practical Solutions to Streaming Glitches on the Fire Stick

- It could be the power source. It needs to be examined for any hardware defect. The power cable and the power adaptor are what am referring to when I say the power source. If it's a bit loose or not securely connected, that's where your buffering originated from. But if that's not the case, you will have to consider other possible causes.

- Another likely cause could be the internet. If you have a slow connection, your streaming will surely be in anarchy. There is a required internet speed for smooth streaming. The user should ensure he has a fast internet connection to prevent buffering of media content while viewing.

- Check the HDMI extension cable. Just like the power cable, if it has any defect or fault, it won't function well and your streaming will keep having interruptions.

So, ensure the cable is in good condition. If it isn't, get it replaced.

- Network could be another cause of poor streaming. This could be due to upgrades or maintenance carried out by the network service provider, external factors like the weather situation too. Nothing can be done here. You simply have to wait it out unless you want to switch to another network.

- It could be storage issues. Simply uninstall apps you don't use or barely use to free up space. Ensure it is space causing the buffering before you proceed.

- If all possible causes are faultless, don't be confused. You simply need to restart your fire stick and the buffering will stop.

Black Screen on the Amazon Fire Stick

Black Screen describes the television set being blank, frozen or refusing to power on. This is a common issue associated with the fire stick over time. I will expose you to the possible causes and feasible solutions for this issue.

Causes of Black Screen

- A possible cause is insufficient power supply. It could be caused by using an incompatible power cord and adaptor.
- When there is no compatibility between the fire stick and your television set.
- Another possible cause is faulty HDMI extension cable. It could be due to a defect like a cut on the cable or the cable not being connected properly to either the fire stick or the television set.
- Incorrect input is the most common cause of the black screen. Incorrect input occurs

when the HDMI cable is inserted into the wrong TV input port.

- Incomplete set up of the fire stick device could also cause a black screen.

How to Solve Black Screen on Fire Stick?

- Detach and reattach the HDMI cable into the port. Also, the user should ensure that he inserts the HDMI cable into the correct HDMI television port to prevent a black screen.
- If your HDMI cable has some sort of impairment, ensure you get that extension cable replaced for a smooth running of the fire stick.
- Ensure to tighten the connection or attachment of the HDMI cable to the television HDMI input port if it's loose.

- Make sure the ports are in perfect condition and get the service of a technician if the fault is detected from the port.
- Use the correct or verified power adapter so enough power supply can be generated for a smooth streaming performance from your fire stick.

What to do if your Fire Stick Doesn't Connect to your Wi-Fi?

This issue could be due to various reasons not limited to; incomplete setup, compatibility issues, password problems. It could be solved by a restart but if it isn't, then you will have to examine what's blocking the connection. Here below are ways this issue can be solved;

- Before anything is done, first verify that nothing is blocking the connection. If affirmative of that, proceed to restart the fire stick device either by remote or physically (by unplugging the power adaptor from the power source). The remote is more convenient, simply navigate to settings, then "Device" then click "restart".

- Examine your Wi-Fi network. This is so you can verify the status of your network and know what to do. You can do this by going to settings, then click "network", then select Play/Pause button on your remote.

- If you are using a laptop or PC, power off your router or modem for some seconds then put it back on.

- Forget your network. Cancelling your fire stick's attempt to connect with your network may help solve the connection issue when you reconnect. To forget your network, simply go to settings, then select "network" then you will see various network options pop up, select "forget network" then "Reconnect". Your problem is solved.

- It could be password problems. Ensure your password is accurate. No omitted character or extra one and no mixing up of either the uppercase or the lower case as passwords are very case sensitive.

- It could also be compatibility issues as well. Fire Stick has certain network and router specifications such as WPA-PSK1 encrypted, WEP, WPA-PSK, open, and hidden networks. It also supports N, B, and G routers on 2.4 GHz, as well as AC, A, and N routers on 5 GHz.

What to do If Your Fire Stick Remote Stops Responding?

- Install the Amazon Fire TV Stick remote app on your device

- If the remote is faulty, get it replaced. New remotes are available on the Amazon online store

- If the remote is fine, then it means the batteries powering it isn't. Get brand new batteries to replace the old ones. If the batteries are still new, remove the batteries and change their positions. Also check that the batteries are well placed. Once all theses are checked, the batteries will begin to work.

How to Resolve Amazon Fire Stick No Signal Error

Did your device suddenly go off while you were streaming on your device and then comes on with a blank screen showing No Signal? Then follow the steps to troubleshoot:

- The HDMI cable has to be tightly fixed to the HDMI port. The cables should not have any cuts.

- Connect the HDMI cable to another HDMI port.

- Use another device to connect to the HDMI port. This would let you know whether the ports are working or not.

- If you confirm that the ports are working, change your cable to the random HDMI cables. It is advisable you use cables that do not have Pin 13 although they are expensive.

- If after trying all these and no improvement, then power off your TV and disconnect the Fire Stick from the HDMI port.

- Put off power on the Fire Stick.

- Allow minimum of 5 to 10 minutes before you restore power to the Fire Stick and leave for another 5 minutes.

- Then put on your TV.
- Plug in the Fire Stick to the HDMI port that is working.
- Then click any button on your Fire Stick remote. Give some seconds interval within each input as it may take about 30 seconds for the device to carry out the inputted command.

What to do if Your Video has no Sound.

Is your TV playing Video but no sound from your Fire Stick device? Then check the following:

- Check the volume settings to ensure that the receiving device is not muted.
- You may switch the audio settings to default as the Fire Stick may not be compatible with the speakers you connected externally.
- Confirm that the audio settings on the TV is correct. Press the Home button to take you to Settings. Tap the Dolby Digital

Output option and confirm that the Dolby Digital Plus is Off.

- Confirm that the HDMI port is working by using the Fire Stick in another device. If the error persists, this means that the HDMI port for your device is faulty.

- What to do when Fire Stick Keeps Restarting

- If your device keeps restarting, then try any of the solutions below:

- It is important to use the Power Cable and block that came with your Fire Stick device. This is because the Fire Stick adapter has some amount of power it gives to your device.

- Change the Micro USB cables if the one you using has stayed for some time.

- You can try to use the 2 Amp Power Adapter. Note that the Fire Stick comes with 1 Amp.

- Let the power adapter be plugged directly to the power outlet.
- Take off all USB extension cable plugged into the Fire Stick Power Adapter.
- Remove any other devices connected to the same TV HDMI port.
- Ensure that your Fire Stick is running the latest version.
- Reset your Fire Stick as the error could be because the device has too many apps installed.
- Change the Television.
- Use the Fire TV remote to restart the Fire Stick.

What to do If your Device isn't Recognizing the Fire Stick

- Confirm that your Fire Stick is fully charged and also check that it is firmly plugged into the TV's HDMI port.

- If you have done the above and there is still no response then the motherboard of the Fire Stick is bad and would need to be replaced.
- How to Resolve 'No Signal' While Installing the Fire Stick?
- Getting this error message while setting up your device? Then follow any of the steps to correct it.
- Be sure that your internet is working as this could be the most reason for this error message. Contact your service provider if your internet is faulty.
- If the internet is working at good speed, then ensure that all the needed connections are well plugged and also plugged tight.
- If you have checked the two above and no improvement, then Remove the router from power for about 15 seconds, then plug back into power.

- If using the Ethernet cable, check that its well connected to the Ethernet port. The cable must be in a good condition without wear and tear.

How to Fix Issues with Images Not Showing

If your Fire Stick device isn't bringing up any image on the screen, do the following:

- Ensure that the HDMI cable is not faulty and is well connected.
- Unplug the cable for some seconds and then reconnect to see if the image would show.
- Replace the HDMI cable if it has shortage.
- If the problem persists, then plug the cable into a different HDMI port in the same TV.
- The problem may have to do with the image resolution. Press and hold both the Rewind and Up buttons at same time for

about 5 seconds. This would switch your device through different image resolution lists. When you get the right resolution, tap "Use Current Resolution"

- If you have tried all the steps above and no change, it means your Fire Stick is faulty and should be changed.

What to do if the Fire TV Stick is not Turning On

- Check that the white indicator light is on. If it is not on, confirm that the power cord in well plugged and firmly inserted at the back of the device.
- If the above doesn't work, then the power cord is most likely damaged. Just replace the cord

Amazing Tips and Tricks for the Fire Stick

Every device has its obvious, normal features and specifications but there is more to a device than it seems on the surface level. There are some fire stick tricks that will definitely be of interest to you. These tricks will help you stream the latest contents for free, use about any Android app, and helps you with your daily activities.

To Have More Choices, Sideload Apps

The Tv's app library is quite limited with the Fire TV Stick. However, you can sideload other apps by manually adding them. Follow the steps below:

- Get to Settings, select System then Developer Options.
- Go to ADB Debugging and click on enable.
- Do same for Apps from Unknown Sources.
- On your phone, download Apps2fire. This file would permit you to install APK files (Android Application Packages) from your phone to the Fire TV.

- When loading large apps, it will take some time due to size. For this reason, change the timing of your phone screen to dim after a minimum of 10 minute so that the app doesn't close.

Use Every Android App on the Fire Stick

By default, the fire stick shouldn't download android apps on the device but with a process called "Sideloading", that default can be bypassed. With the above-mentioned process, it is easy to install Android apps on your device. This is one of the most carried out tricks among users of the Amazon fire TV stick.

Change the Name

Each time you buy a device from Amazon, Amazon gives each device a name. For someone with multiples of same accounts/ devices, this can be quite confusing especially when you need to deliver a purchase to a specific device.

To solve this, just change the name of your devices. Go to "Manage Your Content and Devices Page" under browser. Select your device>click the Edit link. You would see a pop-up window. Here input a name of your choice.

How to Delete Voice Recording.

Amazon store gets to keep record of all the voice search done on the fire TV. If you are concerned about your privacy, you can just delete the voice recordings. Go to "Manage Your Content and Devices Page", select your device, chose Manage Voice Recordings> Delete. To delete the voice searches individually, via the Alexa mobile app, Go to Settings then History, then select an entry of any voice recording, select Delete at the bottom.

Use the Shortcuts

Are you tired of having to go through the Settings option or going through menu just to turn off the Fire Stick? For speedy navigation, hold the home button for some seconds until a pop-up comes on the screen, select Power, Mirroring or Settings.

Using the Amazon Tablet as a Second Screen

You can use the Amazon Fire HDX or HD tablet as a second screen when watching media on the Prime instant or even to navigate on your Fire Stick Device. You also have the option to send media to your tablet and still enjoy your Fire Stick even when the TV is not available. Just go to Settings>Second Screen, then select the ON option. For this to work, both the tablet and the device have to be connected to same wireless connection.

Enjoy Gaming on the Fire Stick with a Gamepad.

Not all titles work well if gaming with the Fire TV's remote. To have more fun gaming on this device, you can get a Fire TV gamepad.

Mirror the Fire Tablet on your TV

You can reflect your Amazon tablet or phone to your TV. First, ensure that both devices are connected to the same wireless connection. Then go to Settings>Displays and Sounds>Display Mirroring on both your tablet and TV.

Use Your Photos as Your Tv's Screen Saver

The Fire Stick device allows you to store your photos in the Amazon cloud as part of the Prime Subscription. To see your picture on your TV as if you seeing it on your phone or laptop, visit Settings under the Amazon Photos app. Choose "Access Amazon Photos," then "Enable Amazon Photos" to view pictures in the Amazon account linked to your Fire TV stick.

Once you are able to access the pictures, you can now play them as slideshow whenever you wish from the Amazon Photos app.

The icing on the cake is having these pictures as a screensaver whenever the TV is on but not in use, Get to Settings>Display and sounds>Screen saver>Album to select the group of pictures you want to play when not using the TV or when playing music from Amazon.

You can also set other things like the duration of each photos on the screen, how the transitions would look, and the time it would take for the screensaver to come on. You can also shuffle the pictures to ensure one picture doesn't repeat.

Switch Off Targeted Advertising

Although most streaming devices allow users to reduce volume of commercials they receive, however it doesn't remove them totally. With Fire TV Stick especially from 5.2.1.1 version, Amazon has made it possible to have your privacy and decide what ads to view or not.

You can choose not to receive interest-based ads, or ads that pop up based on the contents you viewing in different apps. If you watch similar things across different apps, it makes advertisers to keep sending you repeated ads which can be frustrating.

To enjoy more privacy, always update your device to the latest version, then turn off "Interest-based Ads" under Settings.

YouTube for Fire Stick

Although YouTube is not available on the Fire TV Stick officially, but because it runs on Android, it can be gotten into the device. There is a youtube.com icon on the fire Stick but when you click on it, you would be directed to download either Firefox or Silk to continue. Download any of the apps and then you can watch YouTube whenever you want.

After this, once you rap on the YouTube icon, it would take you to the YouTube for TV screen where you can sign in, watch videos as well as sync your YouTube data.

How to Monitor Your Home with the Fire Stick?

This isn't common knowledge but the fire stick can be transformed into a surveillance instrument for the security freaks. All the user has to do is activate the IP camera which transmits still or motion images to a Wi-Fi network. Another smart way of activating the camera is installing the IPCam application on your phone.

Turning Your Phone into a Fire Stick Remote

Anything more convenient than making your own cellular your fire stick remote? I doubt! This is a smart trick for fire stick users to learn. To do this;

- Download the fire stick app on your phone and install. This will serve as an alternative for the voice remote.
- Connect your phone to the same Wi-Fi network as your fire stick.
- A security space will pop up. Enter the 4-digit key.
- Use the voice feature or you could use the screen keyboard to control or navigate your fire stick.

How to Stream Videos from Your Phone or Tablet?

Have you heard of mire cast? If you haven't, it is a means that the fire stick let its users to share its media content on multiple screens or the phone/tablet. Just like the trick above, for this trick to work, you need to connect your phone or tablet to the same network as your fire stick. After that, do the following;

- Go to settings
- Tap the "Display & Sounds" option
- Proceed to "Display mirroring" and enable it
- Then go back, press and hold the home button, options will pop up. Click on "Mirroring"
- Another set of options will show, select "Connect to a Compatible Device".

How to Use Your Fire Stick as a USB Drive?

You can install HD movies to your fire stick since it's a storage device. Due to its portability, you can easily take the device around, plug into a TV and view your movies. Great idea for a hangout.

How to Play Android Games on Your Fire Stick?

To execute this trick, perform the following;

- Go to Google play store, search for App2fire then download on your laptop or PC.
- Now using your fire stick, go to settings menu
- Proceed to "Developer Options", Enable ADB debugging and Apps from unknown sources.
- Go back, head to "About", proceed to "Networks", take note of your IP address.
- After installing the app2fire, go to the setup option on Google play store, this is where you will need to input your IP

address and save. The app is now linked to your fire stick.

- Go back to your computer, search for the game's APK file to download.

- Head to Google play store section, to the local apps. Proceed to click the "Upload/Install from File System" option.

- You will see the APK file you downloaded, upload it here.

- Back to your fire stick, go to ES file explorer, download the app then open the app

- Look at the left side bar, you will see "Downloads" option, click it, you will see the app you installed, click to reinstall. Then proceed to open the app and have fun.

- How to Surf the Net With your Fire Stick?

- You can't stay limited to only streaming services. With this trick, you can browse the internet on your fire stick just as you do on your mobile phone. Install the Fire Fox browser, get a Bluetooth mouse and keypad and you are good to go.

Use Bluetooth Headphones

You can use your preferred headphones to listen to audio on your Fire Stick. To do that, simply connect the headphone through this step:

Settings>Controllers & Bluetooth Devices >Other Bluetooth Devices then choose the Bluetooth device you are connecting to.

How to Put Device to Sleep

On the home screen, hold the home button for 5 seconds to give you a quick pop up to the Settings menu and then press the sleep button to put the device to sleep.

Convert Your Fire Stick to Fire TV Using the USB OTG

Although the Fire Stick is built with OTG functions, however the company do not promote this. To access OTG, make use of hardware designed for it. With the 5$ cable, you can use an OTG on a Fire TV, the cable comes with a male Micro USB jack at the first end and a female micro USB jack at the second end. It also has a female USB type A. To connect, let the male end go into the Fire Stick while the power cable is inserted into the female micro USB jack to act as source of power. Once you are done with the setup, insert a USB thumb drive into the slot for Type A or you can increase the capacity by adding a USB hub before inserting the thumb drive. Go to your file explorer to see the thumb drive.

Let Your Smart Phone be your Keyboard

Typing on the Fire Stick is as painful as the word can be. To avoid this, visit the play store or Apple store to download the Fire TV Remote app and then access it via the Amazon account linked to your Fire Stick. This way you can type on the screen using your phone.

Make your App Home Neat

The current arrangement of apps in the Fire Stick can be messy and confusing. You can arrange the apps in a way that suits you. All you need do is select the apps you want to move and then click on the menu button and click on Move. Now move the apps to any spot you like.

Install the Mouse Toggle

The remote for Fire Stick only allows you move in four directions, left and right, up and down. What happens when you install a browser to surf the net. The solution is installing Mouse Toggle for Fire TV. This app would let you navigate on the screen by introducing a pointer. To install this app, follow the steps below:

- Go to Settings>Device>Developer Options
- Then enable the option of "Allow unknown Sources" and "ADB Debugging".
- Launch the Downloader app. (We already discussed how to install the Downloader app).
- Under Settings in the Developer app, scroll down to Enable JavaScript.
- Return to the Downloader browser tab and enter the URL: https://mytm.pw/mt111
- Next is to click on the Install Mouse Toggle.
- Once the installation is done, click Open
- Select the Enable the mouse service option to have the app start up automatically with the Fire Stick.

- Go to the Home button on the Fire Stick remote for the app to run in the background.
- Once its active, you would see a mouse cursor on the screen to navigate.

How to Use the Ethernet Cable to boost your Internet Speed?

If you experience buffering a lot, this trick is good news for you. Get an Ethernet cable, attach it to your fire stick and do the following;

- Go to settings, click on network settings
- You will see network options, select "Wired" option
- Go back to home and start enjoying fast and smooth streaming.

Jailbreaking the Fire Stick

Although the Amazon Fire TV Stick gives you access to various channels and apps, this comes at a price. Another disadvantage is that you would need multiple paid subscription to be able to get all you want from the various channels and apps.

The only way to solve this is to jailbreak your device which means you would not need to pay before you can watch your preferred movies, shows, live TV etc. Not only is jailbreaking, safe, and simple, it is also very legal. When you jailbreak your device, it would install Kodi on your device which you would use to stream contents on Kodi builds and Kodi Addons. With this, you have an endless access to media contents.

Below are the steps to jailbreak the fire stick;

- Click the "Home" button on your remote to go to the home screen.
- With your remote, go to "Settings", then choose "My Preferences"

- Click "Privacy Settings", disable "Device Data Usage" and "Collect App Usage Data"
- Click "Back" on the remote to leave that section then click "Data Monitoring"
- Disable "Data monitoring"
- Go back to settings menu, click on "Device"
- Click "Developer options", select Apps from Unknown Sources, Click Enable
- Return to the Home Button with your remote.
- Use the Search menu, type Downloader.
- Tap the Download button.
- Open Downloader from the app store once its downloaded.
- Navigate to Settings, then click on Enable JavaScript.
- Type http://tinyurl.com/kodi18rc2 into the downloader app click on the Go button,

then click the Go button again on the Downloader page.

- Allow the file to download on your device.
- Once its downloaded, you get the prompt to Install.
- Go to the bottom of the screen and select the Install option.
- Once done, press **Open.**
- Congratulations! Your fire stick jail break process is complete!

How to Install Kodi On Your Fire Stick?

Installing this application could be a tricky and complicated process. However, the following steps below will guide you in this process;

- Go to settings, then select "Device" option
- Under device settings, select "Developer options" and proceed to enable "apps from unknown sources".

- Then you enable ADB debugging, go back to settings main menu.
- Click "preferences" settings, go to "Advertising ID", disable "interest-based apps".
- Back to main menu again, go to the search bar, type in "Downloader", proceed to download it.
- After downloading, enable the downloader to have access to your media and files.
- Click "Ok" on the next pop up for the quick start guide.
- Open the downloader, go the URL bar and type in: "http://tinyurl.com/kodi18rc2" to commence downloading of Kodi on the fire stick.
- Proceed to install Kodi. Go back to your home screen then navigate to your Apps & games, you will see the Kodi Icon.
- Click it and launch the Kodi app.

Streaming Tips for the Fire Stick

Below are some helpful tips that enables a user easily connect to know how to stream with ease;

- Install the Video & TV Cast Companion app on your fire stick device.
- After installing the app, open your favourite movie or video website in the browser
- Google or enter the movie URL on the browser's address bar
- Wait till the video link is recognized and pops up in the section below the browser window. If nothing happens, play the video and wait for a few seconds.
- Click on "Tap here to Cast" will send the video feed to your Amazon fire TV stick. Have fun!

Movie Tips for the Fire Stick

Are you aware that you can get videos and movies to view for free? Learn how you can amazing contents on your fire stick to watch. Some helpful tips will be outlined below;

Use a virtual private network

Some contents are geographically restricted i.e. they are only available to certain countries. Also, VPN helps secure the user's anonymity and privacy. I strongly advise users to stay away from free VPNs. The recommended VPN for users is IPVanish. It has a particular client that is built as if for the fire stick itself.

Use Free Flix HQ

This video application is very similar in likeness and feel. It comes with amazing features such as being able to select the particular quality of the content you are streaming.

Use Show Box

This "all-in-one" app has a completely different interface from Terrarium TV and Free Flix HQ. The app has a very strong visual aesthetic appeal. It uses large banners for the interface and it gives you a fantastic view of movies and shows on the screen.

Best Apps and Video Services for Your Fire Stick

The fire stick is well known to be an entertainment hub and this is mainly because of its video applications offering fantastic visual entertainment. Here are a good number of apps proven to be the best applications for your fire stick device. They will be your gateway to unlimited entertainment.

1. For Privacy and Secure Streaming

Express VPN

This application is perfect for users who are very concerned about secure internet activities. This application can also be used to view restricted content. Simply change the location of the server to a country where that content is available and accessible. It is easy to install and it is widely regarded as the best network app for the fire stick.

2. For the Best Video Services

A. Kodi

Earlier in this article, a comprehensive guide on how to install this awesome application was outlined. This application serves as an open source for various platforms. It has an amazing interface and it is free to download!

This application gives users an army of options for their entertainment, from music to television shows to full HD movies of different genres. It has also let users share their photos from their personal slideshow.

However, due to heavy surveillance maintained on the users of the app, it is advisable to use a virtual private network to stream on Kodi.

B. Cinema APK

Just like it's counterpart, Kodi, Cinema APK is also free to get to your fire stick. It is a very popular Android application for movies and television shows. This application is credited for having access to several hours of content and an inexhaustible list of contents as well. Yet it doesn't relent there, it keeps getting updated with new releases from time to time. It also gets software updates regularly so it stays trendy and in top condition. It doesn't have original content; it gets content from various servers across the world and it gets quality streams. It is highly recommended for users of the Amazon fire stick.

C. Cyberflix TV

This application functions and looks very similar to the Terrarium TV App which is no surprise as it is a clone of Terrarium TV. The cloning was a result of the shutdown of the Terrarium TV.

It also works like the Cinema APK app. It fetches multiple streams from various sources. It has a solid collection of movies and television shows. It is also free. You sign in your account with the app and have full access to premium and HD content.

It has an efficient quick access system that enables users categorize their content by year, genre and as favourites.

D. Netflix

This is arguably the most popular application for visual entertainment. Unlike the others listed above, it is paid for. Without question, it is one of the best apps for the fire stick.

You get access to content such as "Classics" which is good news for its fans. If you are also a lover of fresh content, Netflix is the app for you.

You can get the app from the Amazon app store and subscribe to it with your fire stick. Another awesome thing about Netflix is that you can use one account on multiple devices.

Also, Netflix has its own virtual private network. Super awesome, right?!

E. MediaBox HD

This application boasts one of the highest demands despite its relatively new entry into mainstream entertainment. It has a huge library of visual content and a user-friendly interface. This application offers high resolution, high quality streams that is why its services are so sought after. It has a feature that lets you sync your view list across various apps and platforms and another feature that features various boxsets from blockbuster movie franchises. Guess what? It is also free.

F. BeeTv

The loveliest thing about this free application is that it boasts of a media collection so huge that you can stream content for several hundreds of hours and you still have so much more left, waiting to be streamed.

It is an aggregator as well, its source links and streams from various servers. The media library is so huge because it gets updated regularly with new content.

G. Crackle

This free video streaming application is a brain child of Sony Entertainment. It contains mostly award-winning contents. But in order to have free access to this content, the user needs to create and login an account on crackle.

Crackle also took the measure to set up parental controls that can be activated if you know you have a child that may want to access contents just like you do. Such controls prevent them from seeing inappropriate content for their age. It has an age filter. This app is available for free on the Amazon app store.

3. For News Services

A. BBC News

This is one of the best apps for the fire stick. It offers services for a specified subscription fee. BBC (British Broadcasting Corporation) boasts a vast network of credible journalists around the world and a global coverage for news reports and correspondence.

With this app, you can read news articles, stream live newscast and it is a vortex of fresh and trendy contents. There are no pop-up ads or commercials to interrupt your use of the app and this is a relief. This application is available on the Amazon App store.

B. Sky News

This app keeps users of the fire stick up to date with events and happenings around the world. It displays its breaking news on the front of your viewing. This way, you don't miss any news update. For lovers of fresh content, it doesn't repeat old news as it regularly drops fresh, hot news constantly. It also has constant weather report updates.

4. For Music

A. Spotify

This app has been a joy giver to music lover around the world. Once you sign in your Spotify account, you get access to millions of songs. With the same Wi-Fi network, you can use a single Spotify account to stream music across multiple devices. That is pretty fantastic. It also gives you a download option so you can download any song that catches your fancy. The app also doesn't bother users with irritable pop-up ads and commercials.

B. YouTube

If you are a smart phone user and you haven't heard of YouTube, then you definitely not on this planet. It is at the forefront of digital entertainment and has an army of addicted consumers.

It is available for download on the Amazon app store. You can search for and play your music and get exposed to new releases. You can also create a playlist for your favourite music and listen to them whenever. The app is free but you will be encountering ads and commercials as you use the application.

5. For Utilities

A. Downloader

This is must-have on your Amazon fire stick. It comes in handy when you want to sideload an application or download your preferred music videos.

This application offers good download speed and helps pause download during a network glitch to prevent corruption of the file in the download process. Due to its high speed, it saves a lot of time. Another feature is that it helps in categorising your newly downloaded files. Follow the steps below to Install this app:

- To start, first visit **Settings** > **Device/My Fire TV** > **Developer** on your Fire Stick.
- Go to **ADB Debugging** and enable.
- Also, activate **Apps from Unknown sources** option.
- Then search for Downloader in the search button on your Fire Stick.
- Once the result is in, select the Downloader application.
- Tap Download to begin to download the app to your device.
- Chose the **Open** button once the download is complete.

B. Mouse Toggle

This utility application enables users to run or use just about any Android application on their fire stick devices. The application puts a cursor on your fire stick screen allowing you to move the cursor while navigating the remote keys. This cursor can reach certain sections in applications that your fire stick remote cannot. This is one of the reasons it is so in demand.

C. Browser

You can install your favourite browser on your fire stick device. It is very useful for the fire stick as it helps you visit the online platforms of other apps and get access to their services without downloading or installing those applications on your fire stick. This way it saves time and space on your fire stick storage. I recommend Fire Fox and Silk.

The Fire OS

The fire operating system is an Android based operating system. The operating system focuses on a personalized user interface, content sourcing, consumption and availability from Amazon application store, Kindle store, Amazon videos, Amazon MP3 and Audible.

The Fire operating system features a "quick access" with categorised apps such as "recently used" and "favourite apps". It also features categorization of applications into different kinds such as apps for games, music, videos, news and utilities in their respective sections.

Unlike other Android devices that comes with pre-installed Google apps such as Google Play store, Google maps and so on, the Fire operating system is exclusively tied to Amazon's software and not Google. It doesn't come with preinstalled apps from Google. The fire operating system is also tied to a content ecosystem.

To get Google apps and APKs into the fire devices such as the fire stick, the apps has to be side-loaded but they still may not be fully compatible with the fire operating system as it is a modified Android operating system.

List of Fire OS Versions

- Android 2.3 (Gingerbread)
- Android 4.0 (Ice Cream Sandwich)
- Android 4.1 (Jelly Bean)
- Android 4.4 (KitKat)
- Android 5.1.1 (Lollipop)
- Android 7.1 (Nougat)

List of Fire OS Devices

- Kindle Fire (HD and HDX)
- Amazon Fire TV
- Amazon Fire TV Stick

- Amazon Fire TV Stick 4k
- Amazon Fire Phone
- Amazon Echo
- Amazon Echo Show
- Amazon Echo Spot

Conclusion

To wrap things up on this user's guide, the Amazon Fire TV Stick is one of the best things to happen to modernization. A progressive step that is ahead of the cable subscription services for television.

All relevant areas concerning the usage of the fire stick has been carefully outlined and discussed in details to make users more familiar with its operations as well as some hidden knowledge Amazon won't want to give away. This user's guide is comprehensive both in content and audience reach. This book has deeply touched everyone's area of interest when it concerns the fire stick device.

If you are pleased with the content of this book, don't forget to recommend this book to a friend.

Thank you.

www.ingramcontent.com/pod-product-compliance
Lightning Source LLC
Chambersburg PA
CBHW031224050326
40689CB00009B/1470